MADONNA

HER COMPLETE STORY

AN UNAUTHORIZED BIOGRAPHY

BY DAVID JAMES

PUBLICATIONS INTERNATIONAL, LTD.

CONTENTS

"LUCKY STAR"
Madonna's Early Life

Madonna Louise Veronica Ciccone, the Michigan high school girl who would eventually shake up the world.

BORN ON AUGUST 16, 1959, IN BAY City, Michigan, Madonna Louise Veronica Ciccone was the third and eldest daughter in a lower-middle class family of six children. When she was just six years old, Madonna lost her mother (whom she was named after) to breast cancer. She firmly believes this had a profound effect on the way her own life turned out.

"When my mother died, all of a sudden I was going to become the best student, get the best grades," she told *US* magazine. "I was going to become the best singer, the best dancer, the most famous person in the world. Everybody was going to love me."

After her mother's death, Madonna was constantly vying for papa Sylvio's attention. Consequently, when the Chrysler engineer remarried a couple of years later, his eldest daughter wasn't happy and she admits being resentful toward her stepmother.

Madonna's upbringing was a strict Catholic one—most days she was forced to rise at six or seven in the morning to

Madonna (center) shows 'em some style during her days as a high school cheerleader.

"I SOMETIMES THINK I WAS BORN TO LIVE UP TO MY NAME. HOW COULD I BE ANYTHING ELSE BUT WHAT I AM HAVING BEEN NAMED MADONNA? I WOULD EITHER HAVE ENDED UP A NUN OR THIS."

Madonna; *Vanity Fair,* **1991**

attend church before going to school. Ultimately, she began to rebel against her religion, both at home and at school.

As a youngster, Madonna developed a passion for dancing. In addition to becoming a cheerleader, she took ballet classes while attending Rochester Adams High School. During this period, she reportedly found a mentor in dance instructor Christopher Flynn, who held classes at his own school. Flynn has been credited by Madonna for giving her the confidence to really break out on her own. During an interview with the *Advocate*, Madonna declared that a pivotal point in her adolescence was when Flynn took her dancing to a gay club in Detroit.

"In school and in my neighborhood and everything, I felt like such an outsider, a misfit, a weirdo. And suddenly when I went to that club I didn't feel that way anymore. . . . I had a whole new sense of myself."

On graduating from Rochester Adams High, Madonna won a scholarship to the University of Michigan. However, she decided to quit after five semesters and get into the groove of New York City. Her goals? "I wanted to dance. I wanted to sing. I wanted to make people happy. I wanted to be famous. I wanted everybody to love me. I wanted to be a star. I worked very hard . . . and my dream came true."

By the time she reached New York City, Madonna's cheerleader persona was just a distant memory.

"INTO THE GROOVE"

Madonna's Music

I'VE WRITTEN MY BEST

THINGS WHEN I'M UPSET, BUT THEN WHO

HASN'T? WHAT'S THE POINT OF SITTING DOWN

AND NOTATING YOUR HAPPINESS?"

Madonna; *Rolling Stone, 1991*

Madonna's success as a recording artist is almost unprecedented in the music business. Much of this success is due to the star's shrewd cultivation of multiple personas. Just two of many are on these pages.

WHEN MADONNA RELEASED HER greatest-hits package, *The Immaculate Collection*, toward the end of 1990, world-wide sales of her album catalog were estimated at a staggering 75 million units. More remarkable, perhaps, is that such impressive sales figures were accrued in just over seven years. When Madonna's self-titled debut album hit the streets in July 1983, few could have predicted that it would mark the beginning of an amazing megaplatinum recording career.

At that juncture, landing an album contract with a major record label must have been a big enough deal in itself for Madonna. After all, when she first signed with Sire Records in 1982, only a couple of 12-inch dance singles were guaranteed. The company waited to see how these fared before giving her the green light to go in and cut a complete album.

Madonna never looked back once she connected with Sire, but it had taken her several years to find her musical niche after arriving in New York during the late '70s. She spent a brief period in Paris,

Right and above: Even as early as during photo sessions to promote her first album, Madonna established that she was a woman of more than one mood and image.

> "POP SONGS ARE REALLY EASY TO WRITE. MICHAEL JACKSON'S BEEN WORKING ON HIS ALBUM FOR LIKE THREE YEARS. I CAN'T IMAGINE ANY-ONE DOING THAT! I'D GO INSANE."
>
> **Madonna;** *Rolling Stone,* 1991

lured by a couple of producers who promised to make her the proverbial star. But Madonna soon turned her back on the City of Lights and returned to New York, where she learned to play guitar and drums while dating musician Dan Gilroy. Those early musical lessons paved the way for Madonna's year-long stint drumming alongside Gilroy and his brother Ed in their band, the Breakfast Club.

When Madonna quit the Gilroys, ex-Michigan boyfriend Stephen Bray became her principal songwriting partner. After a stint with a dubious management organization, she and Bray cut a series of demos that included "Everybody" and "Burning Up." Both songs would end up on her first album.

However, in order to really break into the business, Madonna decided she had to go it alone. Consequently, she started hanging out and making contacts in Manhattan dance clubs like the Roxy and Danceteria. At the latter club, she hooked up with in-house DJ Mark Kamins. Recognizing her potential, Kamins

reworked some of her demos and then presented them to Sire Records.

As soon as Sire had given Madonna the go-ahead, she started cutting her debut album, *Madonna,* at New York's Sigma Sound studios. She had allegedly promised both Mark Kamins and Stephen Bray that they would produce the album. Kamins's version of "Everybody" made the final record, but she ended up cutting most of the tracks with producer Reggie Lucas.

In addition to handling some of the mixes, Madonna's new boyfriend, DJ John "Jellybean" Benitez, produced "Holiday," a tune he had found for her. "Holiday" became the album's leadoff single, but it

The Madonna *album established the star's unique qualities of personality: desirable yet intriguingly scruffy, independent yet available.*

initially failed to take off in the way that both artist and label might have hoped.

While "Holiday" eventually became a Top 10 hit toward the end of 1983, it was the Lucas-penned "Borderline" and its accompanying video that fueled the debut album's lift-off. By early 1984, sales of *Madonna* had increased dramatically and would continue to escalate through the year. The single "Lucky Star" reached number four on *Billboard*'s Hot 100 in October; by the end of the year, Madonna's debut had been certified double platinum in recognition of its two-million-plus sales.

The launch of Madonna's second album, *Like a Virgin*, was delayed as Sire allowed her debut release to run its course. The new record finally hit the streets in November 1984 and was an instant smash. By year's end, Madonna had scored her first number one hit (and gold single) with the title track, which took just five weeks to reach the top spot.

At the production helm for *Like a Virgin* was Nile Rodgers, whose midas touch had previously worked wonders for the likes of David Bowie and Duran Duran. To back Madonna, he recruited a posse of top New York session players, including Bernard Edwards and Tony Thompson, both of whom Rodgers had worked with during the late '70s in the legendary New York disco outfit Chic.

Interestingly, Rodgers had initially balked at the idea of recording the song "Like a Virgin." Although he liked the

melody, he told the *Los Angeles Times*, "I didn't think the lyric 'like a virgin' was such a terrific hook." Four days later, unable to get the song out of his head, the producer conceded to his artist that the Tom Kelly/Billy Steinberg song could well be a hit. For her part, Madonna claims she knew it was a smash the moment she heard it, despite the fact that Steinberg had never intended his lyrics to be sung by a female!

NOT MANY NEW RECORDING ARTISTS CAN HIT A HOME RUN THEIR FIRST TIME AT BAT, BUT THAT'S WHAT MADONNA DID WITH HER FIRST LP, WHICH WENT DOUBLE PLATINUM IN 1984.

The *Like a Virgin* LP also spawned the hit singles "Material Girl," "Angel," and "Dress You Up." Additionally, during the first half of 1985, Madonna scored with three movie-oriented songs—"Crazy For You" and "The Gambler" from the film *Vision Quest*, and "Into the Groove" from *Desperately Seeking Susan*.

In its first year of release, *Like a Virgin* sold more than six million copies.

Madonna had arrived.

Madonna fans had to wait until the summer of 1986 before the emergence of her third studio album, *True Blue*. Taking

Above and opposite: Record buyers responded to Madonna's music, but they were particularly intrigued by her image of streetwise sass. Her bare midriff, funky costume jewelry, and "I-don't-care" attitude helped turn the Madonna LP into a success.

To record buyers of an earlier era, Madonna's upfront sexuality may have seemed brazen, but to her fans—particularly young women— she seemed to sum up the importance of taking charge of one's own life.

a stronger role in the writing and production, this record saw her collaborating with old friend Stephen Bray and Pat Leonard, the musical director on her Virgin Tour.

Once again, Madonna came up with a winner. She scored two out-of-the-box number one hits with "Live To Tell" (the theme song for hubby Sean Penn's movie, *At Close Range*) and the controversial "Papa Don't Preach." Madonna had been well aware that the subject matter of the latter tune would cause tongues to wag, as she explained to *The New York Times*:

"It is a message song that everyone is going to take the wrong way. Immediately they're going to say I am advising every young girl to go out and get pregnant

... to me, it's a celebration of life.'

In February 1987 Madonna topped the charts with "Open Your Heart." Two more singles from the album—the title song and "La Isla Bonita"—reached the Top 5 before it had run its course.

By August of 1987, *True Blue* had sold five million copies.

Madonna topped the *Billboard* singles chart for the sixth time (more than any other artist in the '80s) during the third week of August 1987 with the theme song for her latest movie, "Who's That Girl?" The soundtrack album of the same title was certified platinum two months after its release, but it probably wasn't what her fans were hoping for.

Madonna contributed just four songs to the package, two collaborations with Stephen Bray and two with Pat Leonard. The rest of the set comprised tracks by the likes of Club Nouveau, Scritti Politti, and Coati Mundi. Still, Madonna continued to sustain her chart momentum, riding high with "The Look Of Love" and "Causing A Commotion."

Dance remix albums can hardly be considered a rarity these days, with many multiplatinum artists such as Paula Abdul, Bobby Brown, and New Kids on the Block getting in on the action. However, Madonna broke fresh ground when she assembled the *You Can Dance* package for the 1987 holiday season. With the exception of one new song, "Spotlight," the album featured extended versions of Madonna's more dance-oriented hits.

It should be noted that this was the first Madonna album to contain a version of her 1985 club smash, "Into The Groove." Previously, the record was only available on the B-side of the 12-inch version of "Angel."

"With *Like a Prayer*, Madonna doesn't ask to be taken seriously, she insists on it." That's what *Rolling Stone* had to say in its review of Madonna's first full-length studio album in almost three years. Unquestionably her most introspective work to date, Madonna described the album as "an assimilation of experiences I've had in my life and in my relationships . . . the pain of dying, of growing up and letting go."

Family and religion and, more specifically, the death of her mother and her recent divorce from Sean Penn were among the themes that the singer broached on the record.

Left and above: *Madonna quickly established that hip, fashionable looks don't have to cost a fortune.*

"*. . . LIKE A PRAYER* IS PROOF NOT ONLY THAT MADONNA SHOULD BE TAKEN SERIOUSLY AS AN ARTIST, BUT THAT HERS IS ONE OF THE MOST COMPELLING VOICES OF THE '80s."

Like a Prayer album review; *Rolling Stone*, 1989

"My first couple of albums I would say came from the little girl in me, who is interested only in having people like me, in being entertaining and charming and frivolous and sweet," Madonna told *Interview*. "And this new one is the adult side of me, which is concerned with being brutally honest."

In addition to the leadoff title track, *Like a Prayer* spawned a succession of hit singles, including "Express Yourself," "Cherish," "Oh Father," and "Keep It

According to Madonna, singing Sondheim material wasn't easy. "They're very difficult songs to learn," she told *Interview*. "I mean, one song is written with five sharps. They're brilliant, but really complex, though."

In addition to the Sondheim material, the *Dick Tracy* album boasted six songs co-written by Madonna, including the Top 10 hit "Hanky Panky."

Together." Once again, her principal musical collaborators were Bray and Leonard.

Madonna dedicated *Like a Prayer* to the memory of her mother. The record's overriding somber vibe was underlined by the star's decision to provide an insert on the facts about AIDS in every copy.

How the dancefloor smash "Vogue" could possibly have had any connection whatsoever with the *Dick Tracy* movie will remain an eternal mystery. Still, when the single was released at the end of March 1990, it was an instant hit and ranks as Madonna's biggest seller to date. Its inclusion on her *I'm Breathless: Music From and Inspired by the Movie Dick Tracy* album no doubt helped sell a few copies of the record, but it really was quite out of context with any of the LP's other material. Madonna sang three tunes written by acclaimed Broadway composer Stephen Sondheim, including the Academy Award-winning "Sooner Or Later."

MADONNA'S BEST-OF COMPILATION, *THE IMMACULATE COLLECTION*, PROVED TO BE THE RECORD EVERYBODY WANTED FOR CHRISTMAS, 1990. MADONNA FANS CONSIDERED IT ESSENTIAL.

Released on November 13, 1990, the best-of collection called *The Immaculate Collection* featured 15 of Madonna's biggest hits, as well as two new songs, "Justify My Love" and "Rescue Me." Two million copies of the album were sold over the holiday season and both of the newly recorded tunes became chart hits.

A strong package, though there were some notable omissions that prevented it from becoming the definitive Madonna collection. These included "Dress You Up," "Angel," "Oh Father," "Keep It Together," and songs from the *Who's That Girl?* sessions.

Diehard fans anxious for *The Compleat Madonna* will probably have to wait a few years for the boxed set! And wait they will, for Madonna has proved herself a versatile performer whose recording career shows every promise of being a long one—particularly when judged by the capricious standards of pop music. Madonna's records continue to excite fans and sell in great numbers. That's a tribute not only to her musicianship and ability to select solid material, but to her ability to use her music to communicate with her listeners in subtle, even intimate, ways. As fiery as they are danceable, Madonna's recordings mark her as a powerfully unique talent. There seems little doubt that the best is yet to come.

ALBUM DISCOGRAPHY

1983
MADONNA (Sire)

"Lucky Star," "Borderline," "Burning Up," "I Know It," "Holiday," "Think of Me," "Physical Attraction," "Everybody"

1984
LIKE A VIRGIN (Sire)

"Material Girl," "Angel," "Like a Virgin," "Over and Over," "Love Don't Live Here Anymore," "Dress You Up," "Shoo-Bee-Doo," "Pretender," "Stay"

1986
TRUE BLUE (Sire)

"Papa Don't Preach," "Open Your Heart," "White Heat," "Live to Tell," "Where's the Party," "True Blue," "La Isla Bonita," "Jimmy Jimmy," "Love Makes the World Go Round"

1987
YOU CAN DANCE (Sire)

"Spotlight," "Holiday," "Everybody," "Physical Attraction," "Spotlight" (dub version), "Holiday" (dub version), "Over and Over," "Into the Groove," "Where's the Party," "Over and Over" (dub version), "Into the Groove" (dub version)

1989
LIKE A PRAYER (Sire)

"Like a Prayer," "Express Yourself," "Love Song," "Till Death Do Us Part," "Promise to Try," "Cherish," "Dear Jessie," "Oh Father," "Keep It Together," "Spanish Eyes," "Act of Contrition"

1990
I'M BREATHLESS: MUSIC FROM AND INSPIRED BY THE FILM DICK TRACY (Sire)

"He's a Man," "Sooner or Later," "Hanky Panky," "I'm Going Bananas," "Cry Baby," "Something to Remember," "Back in Business," "More," "What Can You Lose," "Now I'm Following You (Part I)," "Now I'm Following You (Part II)," "Vogue"

1990
THE IMMACULATE COLLECTION (Sire)

"Holiday," "Lucky Star," "Borderline," "Like a Virgin," "Material Girl," "Crazy for You," "Into the Groove," "Live to Tell," "Papa Don't Preach," "Open Your Heart," "La Isla Bonita," "Like a Prayer," "Express Yourself," "Cherish," "Vogue," "Justify My Love," "Rescue Me"

Opposite: In less than a decade, Madonna has put together a substantial body of recorded work. Fiercely dedicated to her music and intimately involved in every detail of its creation, she seems poised for continued musical growth.

"BURNING UP"

Madonna's Videos

T HE SEXUALITY IN MY VIDEOS IS

ALL CONSENTED TO—NO ONE'S TAKING

ADVANTAGE OF EACH OTHER."

Madonna; *Advocate,* **1991**

Madonna's videos are an important—and often controversial—part of her career. Though roundly criticized in some quarters for their explicitness, the videos have been honored with industry awards, and have certainly fueled record sales.

ON NOVEMBER 27, 1990, THE HOT news in the entertainment world was that MTV would *not* be airing the new Madonna video, "Justify My Love." Because the video featured frank sexual imagery, MTV executives clearly felt that Madonna had gone too far this time and that "Justify My Love" was simply too hot to handle.

Madonna could not have bought better publicity. The day the MTV ban was reported, the media went into overdrive, with network and cable news programs scrambling to run stories and air "edited" footage from the video. *Saturday Night Live* dared to run most of the clip. A couple of nights later, *Nightline* aired a complete version, followed by a live satellite interview with Madonna herself. Over the ensuing days, newspapers and magazines were quick to jump on the bandwagon, documenting both the story of the MTV ban and its hurricane-like effect on the broadcast media. In less than a week, "Justify My Love" had been promoted in more households than it could ever have hoped to reach with a standard MTV exclusivity deal.

And just to ensure that her fans did not miss out on the action, the good folks at Warner-Reprise home video announced that a specially priced $9.98 video single of the song would be in stores by December 6—the perfect stocking stuffer for every Madonna fan. Two months later, in February 1991, that video single became the first-ever short-form clip to be certified multiplatinum for sales of more than 400,000 copies.

Clearly, MTV had done Madonna a tremendous favor by banning "Justify My Love." Many cynics suggested that the whole affair had been a cleverly conceived marketing ploy by the Madonna camp. However, both the artist and her associates vigorously denied such accusations. Whatever the case, the whole "Justify My Love" scenario not only proved Madonna's ongoing ability to cause a good commotion, but it also confirmed that she is unquestionably the ultimate video star. When Madonna makes a video, people want to see it, period. And with the exception, perhaps, of Michael Jackson, no other artist has such amazing video appeal.

In many respects, Madonna is the First Lady of the MTV era. When she initially started making video clips to support her early recordings in 1982, the MTV video network was barely a year old. And while other multiplatinum female artists have emerged on the video scene during the past decade, Madonna will always be forever MTV's girl—bans or no bans.

Madonna's personal video history dates back to the early '80s, when she made a couple of low-budget clips for the singles "Everybody" and "Burning Up." However, it was in 1983, with the Mary Lambert-directed clip for "Borderline," that Madonna really connected with the MTV scene. In "Borderline" we watched her hanging out in lower Manhattan with a spray can gang. In the subsequent "Lucky Star" the young singer quickly found a following among girls who fell for her streetwise looks, charm, and attitude, and among guys who just figured she was cool enough to hang out with.

The budgets had been fairly modest for the videos for songs from Madonna's first album, but little expense was spared when it came to shooting the leadoff single and title track for her second album, "Like a Virgin." Under the watchful eye of director Mary Lambert, the young starlet traveled to Venice during the summer of '84. Baring her belly button and sporting the now legendary "Boy Toy" belt buckle, Madonna cavorted her way through the Venetian canals on a gondola; conceptual scenes had her roaming around with a lion-masked human hunk and with a real-life king of the jungle.

Next up was "Material Girl," in which Lambert helped Madonna pay tribute to the late Marilyn Monroe's "Diamonds Are a Girl's Best Friend" number from the movie *Gentlemen Prefer Blondes*. Not surprisingly, the clip inspired comparisons of Madonna and Monroe. Some of the

tabloids even ran stories suggesting that Madonna believed she was a reincarnation of the '50s sex symbol.

"At first I enjoyed the comparisons between me and her," Madonna would tell *Rolling Stone*. "I saw it all as a compliment . . . then it started to annoy me, because nobody wants to be continuously compared to someone else. You want people to see that you have a statement of your own to make." The Material Girl concluded, "Marilyn Monroe was a victim and I'm not. That's why there's really no comparison."

In addition to the first two "Virgin" clips, the first half of 1985 saw MTV airing a clip for "Into The Groove," which comprised scenes from her movie *Desperately Seeking Susan*. The final video employed to promote the second album was an in-concert clip of "Dress You Up," taken from the home video concert tape.

After working with Mary Lambert on a number of vidclips, Madonna opted for a change on the first couple of singles from her 1986 *True Blue* album. The leadoff single was "Live To Tell," the theme from the movie *At Close Range*, an intense thriller that starred Christopher Walken and Madonna's then-husband Sean Penn. Since the video for this song was closely linked with the movie, it was hardly surprising that the film's director, James Foley, handled the clip.

Madonna clearly enjoyed working with Foley. Their collaborative efforts continued on the follow-up single, "Papa

Opposite and above: Madonna was not only an early player in the music-video revolution—she very nearly defined this new tool of art and salesmanship. As these early images suggest, Madonna wasted no time in establishing a powerful video presence.

Don't Preach." The basic storyline for "Papa" revolved around a close-cropped, blonde-haired Italian teenager (Madonna) with an unexpected pregnancy who seeks the approval of her father (actor Danny Aiello). However, there was also some stylish performance footage in which Madonna made sure the world could see she'd been working out heavily. No longer was Madonna a streetwise "tramp"—her brand of sex appeal was now much more sophisticated.

An additional two videos were shot to support the *True Blue* album—"Open Your Heart" and "La Isla Bonita." The former was directed by Jean-Baptiste Mondino and was arguably Madonna's most sexually oriented effort to date. Set in a kind of futuristic peep show, the video allowed the skimpily attired star to gyrate to the rhythm of the music in the manner of a stripper or go-go dancer.

Director Mary Lambert was back at the helm for "La Isla Bonita," which was much more serene than the "Open Your Heart" clip. On the image front, Madonna's hair was dark and slicked-back for most of the scenes, although she did let her locks down for some Spanish senorita-style street segments.

Crucifixes have long been a feature in Madonna videos, but their imagery has never been employed more often or more potently than in the first single and title track of her 1989 album, *Like a Prayer*, where she danced in a field of blazing crosses a la the movie *Mississippi Burning*.

"I LIKE THE CHALLENGE OF MERGING ART AND COMMERCE. AS FAR AS I'M CONCERNED, MAKING A VIDEO IS ALSO A COMMERCIAL."

Madonna; *Rolling Stone*, **1989**

The Mary Lambert-directed "Prayer" video, which contained strong religious imagery throughout, was originally set to run in tandem with Madonna's first commercial for Pepsi, part of a reported $5 million sponsorship tie-in with the soft drink company.

"The treatment for the video is a lot more controversial [than in the commericial]," Madonna told *Interview*. "It's probably going to touch a lot of nerves in a lot of people. And the treatment for the commercial is . . . very, very sweet. It's very sentimental."

In the Pepsi spot Madonna was seen reliving a childhood birthday party. However, after the two-minute clip aired during a March 2 segment of *The Cosby Show*, Pepsi was immediately forced to yank it from the airwaves. Indeed, such was the outrage from religious and cultural groups, which viewed Madonna's MTV clip as "totally blasphemous," that the soft-drink company completely severed its sponsorship ties with the singer.

"Like a Prayer" was undeniably Madonna's most controversial video outing to date. Now, more than ever, she recognized her power to generate attention through the medium. What better way to follow the "Prayer" video than with the highly erotic "Express Yourself"? In a *Rolling Stone* interview, Madonna stated that the David Fincher-directed clip "showed an extreme. First you see me chained to a bed, then you see me on top of a stairway with these working men below . . . ."

Get the picture? For the next single, "Cherish," Madonna spent a day at the beach with longtime photographer friend Herb Ritts. He shot a stylish black-and-white clip of Madonna rolling in the sea and sand in a surf-soaked dress, while a school of male mermaids swam through the ocean.

Madonna stayed in black and white as she reunited with David Fincher for the reflective "Oh Father" video, which offered *Citizen Kane*/Rosebud-style glimpses of a young girl dealing with a death in the family.

Although never broadcast in the U.S., an animated video for the song "Dear Jessie" (from the *Like a Prayer* album) was distributed overseas, where it was released as a single. The clip reportedly featured lots of pink elephants and a cartoon version of Madonna.

"Vogue," arguably Madonna's most stylized video to date, premiered on MTV during the spring of 1990 and was a black-and-white delight that comprised wonderful images of the singer, backed by a troop of voguers. The superstar gave

her fans an open view of her chest during scenes in which she wore a see-through top. Interestingly, the moral MTV mob let her get away with it—after all, ratings are ratings!

As 1990 drew to a close, "Justify My Love" emerged on the scene. Shot at the Royal Monceau hotel in Paris, the video was described by *Entertainment Weekly* as "a montage of steamy, hypererotic images that make Madonna's past forays into video kink look about as racy as This Old House." Enough said.

Most of Madonna's video work is available on home video. Following its 1985 release of four early clips in a short-form package, Warner-Reprise has issued concert videos from the Virgin and Who's That Girl tours, the 1990 best-of "Immaculate Collection," and the "Justify My Love" clip. Meanwhile, the final date of the Blond Ambition Tour is available on laserdisc through Pioneer.

Controversy shadows Madonna's every move. Her "Rock the Vote" video, done to pull young people to the polls, raised the ire of many people, who objected to Madonna's provocative use of the American flag.

"SPOTLIGHT"
Madonna In Concert & On Stage

I REALLY DEFY ANYONE

NOT TO SUCCUMB TO IT. NONSTOP

ENERGY! IT FULFILLS MY NAME

FOR HER—BUZZBOMB!"

**Warren Beatty, after seeing Madonna's
Blond Ambition show;** *Rolling Stone,* **1990**

*Whether getting down at the Live
Aid concert (left) or preening in period garb for the MTV Awards (opposite), Madonna is always a sensation
in concert and on stage.*

24

"I THINK I OFFEND CERTAIN GROUPS [BUT] I THINK THAT PEOPLE WHO UNDERSTAND WHAT I'M DOING AREN'T OFFENDED BY IT."

Madonna, MTV

This page: Madonna's Virgin Tour featured the star in a variety of provocative outfits and attitudes. Not surprisingly, the tour was a sellout.

DESPITE THE FACT THAT MADONNA has performed in front of thousands —no, make that millions—of people during her career, it was fascinating to observe her hands visibly shaking as she started to sing "Sooner Or Later" (from the movie *Dick Tracy*) at the 1991 Academy Awards ceremony. Was she uneasy at being face-to-face with Hollywood's finest? Or did she suddenly panic with the realization that television viewers around the world would be scrutinizing her performance? Whatever the case, it was reassuring to discover that even Madonna gets the occasional case of the butterflies.

Fortunately for the blonde bombshell—that was her hair color on March 25—she soon hit her stride during her Oscar-ceremony performance and ended up delivering a fine rendition of the Stephen Sondheim tune. And when the composer received one of those coveted golden statuettes later in the evening, Madonna's nervous start was largely forgotten by the audience.

The word "nervous" is, of course, not one that is generally associated with Madonna. Only six months earlier, she climaxed her marathon 1990 Blond Ambition tour with a sellout show at a giant outdoor stadium in Nice on the French Riviera that was beamed via satellite to U.S. cable viewers. During that two-hour, 18-song performance, it seemed that she had the world in the palm of her hand.

Madonna has certainly come a long

way since her teens, when she used to beg then-boyfriend and drummer Stephen Bray to allow her on stage to dance during his band's sets in Michigan clubs. But, then again, everyone has to start somewhere . . . .

Although she would ultimately find fame and fortune as a singer, Madonna cut her musical teeth behind a drum kit, when she connected with the Gilroy brothers in their New York band, the Breakfast Club. Following a year-long stint playing "just about every dive on [Manhattan's] Lower East Side," Madonna decided that she had to be in the spotlight. Consequently, after reconnecting with Bray (who had moved to the Big Apple), Madonna sang while he played drums in a variety of Gotham-based

pop/rock bands such as the Millionaires, Modern Dance, and Emmy.

By the time Madonna had acquired a taste for more dance-oriented rhythms and had signed her 1982 deal with Sire Records, she no longer needed a backing band. As a "track artist," she would either lip-sync or sing over pre-recorded backing tapes. To sustain visual interest, Madonna incorporated a couple of male dancers into her act.

It wasn't until the spring of 1985 that Madonna made her return to conventional live performing when she embarked on her first national concert dates, dubbed the Virgin Tour. A memorable performance of "Like A Virgin" at the 1984 MTV Awards show at New York's Radio City Music Hall, where Madonna writhed

The Virgin Tour was Madonna's first set of national concert dates. At every stop, her performances were characterized by plenty of infectious energy and style.

around the stage clad in a white wedding dress and some sexy lingerie, had whetted appetites for her concerts. And with sales of her first two albums skyrocketing, it wasn't surprising that all 38 dates on the Virgin Tour were instant sellouts.

Pat Leonard, who had just finished working with the Jacksons, was enlisted as Madonna's musical director. He had initially turned down the gig, but after being "charmed" by the singer during a two-hour phone conversation, he agreed to put her band together. To this day, Leonard remains one of Madonna's closest musical collaborators.

The Virgin Tour kicked off in Seattle, and by the time it had concluded some three months later, Madonna had performed to more than 300,000 fans at mainly mid-size, theatrical venues. Although Leonard had assembled a strong

Both pages: The Who's That Girl Tour took Madonna to three continents. Each 100-minute show was sensational, and put Madonna into a variety of sexy costumes.

"I CALL THE TOUR WHO'S THAT GIRL BECAUSE I PLAY A LOT OF CHARACTERS. AND EVERY TIME I DO A VIDEO OR A SONG, PEOPLE GO, 'OH, THAT'S WHAT SHE'S LIKE.' AND I'M NOT LIKE ANY OF THEM. I'M ALL OF THEM. I'M NONE OF THEM. YOU KNOW WHAT I MEAN?"

Madonna; *Rolling Stone*, 1987

backing band, most of the attention was firmly focused on Madonna and her sexy stage antics. As *People Weekly* reported, "She writhes, wiggles, shimmies her semi-liquid assets and gleefully misbehaves. No female rocker (except perhaps Tina Turner in her Ike days) ever whipped up such an erotic frenzy."

Above and right: A high point of the Who's That Girl Tour was Madonna's "Like a Virgin"/ "Material Girl" medley.

The audiences comprised a large number of young female fans, dubbed "Madonna-Wannabes," who showed up at concerts emulating their idol's raunchy image. Suffice it to say that during 1985 Madonna did more for the lingerie industry than any Madison Avenue ad campaign could have ever achieved.

In addition to spending their money on looking like Madonna, the "Wannabes" snapped up just about every piece of Madonna merchandise they could get their hands on. Official merchandiser Dell Furano claimed that the Material Girl was doing better business than Bruce Springsteen, the Rolling Stones, and even British teen heroes Duran Duran. Indeed, at a San Francisco date, Furano estimated that sales of $20 Madonna T-shirts averaged one every six seconds.

Following an emotional return to her Detroit hometown for a show at Cobo Hall, Madonna finally climaxed the Virgin Tour with a sellout concert at New York's prestigious Madison Square Garden. (Earlier in the tour, she had sold out three shows at Radio City Music Hall.) During the Garden performance, she told the 19,000-strong crowd that she used to live near the venue and had often dreamed of one day being a headliner there. During an interview with *Rolling Stone*, old friend Stephen Bray remembered Madonna's former address, and confirmed that this was indeed a true story: "It was one of those little rooming houses where you'd walk in and it would

Fans enjoyed Madonna's willingness to spoof her sexy image by appearing in this hilariously awful outfit.

smell [and] I'd say 'I'm not coming here to visit you again.' Then she was living for a while between Avenues A and B [on the Lower East Side] and I always thought I was gonna be killed by junkies . . . ."

Madonna's rise to the top had certainly been meteoric, to say the least. However, as she celebrated her recording and concert triumphs, the past came back to haunt her in the form of a series of nude photographs taken in 1979, and acquired six years later by *Penthouse* and *Playboy* magazines. Both magazines hit the

Madonna's matted hair tells the story of how hard she worked to please her fans during the Who's That Girl Tour.

minds. And just in case anyone needed reminding, Bette Midler sarcastically introduced her by saying, "Here's a woman who pulled herself up by her bra straps and who has been known to let them down occasionally."

It was a potentially disastrous moment, but the way Madonna handled the Live Aid audience marked a significant point in her career as a performer. Clad stylishly (and modestly) in a long coat, offering no hint of a bra strap or belly button, she delighted the crowd with renditions of "Into The Groove" and "Holiday." And, rather than shy away from the topic that was on everyone's mind, she faced it head on. She announced to the crowd that she would not be removing any of her clothing during the show because "I don't want you to hold it against me in 10 years."

The crowd loved her upfront attitude and Madonna learned an invaluable lesson, as she later told Q magazine. "I decided to be a warrior and it worked. And that was the first time that I had really understood my power."

Almost two years would pass before Madonna would once again exercise that power over concert audiences. She pretty much avoided live performances in 1986, limiting her stage work that year to a few New York performances in a Lincoln Center workshop play called *Goose and Tomtom*. Critics were not invited to

streets during the second week of July 1985, just days before Madonna was set to play the biggest concert of her career thus far—the U.S. segment of Live Aid at Philadelphia's JFK Stadium.

With a crowd of 90,000 in attendance at the Philly stadium and millions of fans watching the global television broadcast, Madonna was understandably nervous about going on stage knowing that everybody would have the nudie pix on their

This page: Humor, intensity, passion—Madonna served up all of that and much more during the Who's That Girl dates.

This page: Much of the look of Madonna's Blond Ambition tour was created by designer Jean-Paul Gaultier, whose sexy costumes pushed Madonna into a new realm.

attend. As a result, press coverage was minimal.

Nineteen-eighty-seven was the year of the Who's That Girl Tour, which saw Madonna performing to an estimated two million concertgoers on three continents. Because many of the performances had been booked into outdoor stadiums, the challenge for Madonna was to create a spectacular show. As she explained to writer Mikal Gilmore during the tour's opening leg in Japan, "The challenge was being able to make a show interesting in a stadium, where you're not supposed to be interesting, where it's like just this mega-big show, real impersonal. I wanted to make it really personal, even though people would be sitting really far away from

me. And I think that's what we've managed to do."

In order to create the Who's That Girl show, a state-of-the-art stage production was created. Featured were a giant stairway, several levels of moving floors, and huge screens on which videos and other images could be projected.

Once again, Pat Leonard was musical director/keyboardist. He was accompanied by six-piece band, with three backing vocalists also in tow. Additionally, the show used three dancers, including choreographer Shabba Doo and teenager Chris Finch.

"Who's That Girl" was a particularly apt tour name, for Madonna underwent a variety of changes in costume and image

This page: Blond Ambition was a highly theatrical show that was more akin to a Broadway production than a pop concert. By this time, Madonna's versatility and willingness to experiment had set her apart from other pop stars.

during each 100-minute performance. On a vocal level, she showed tremendous maturity in her singing abilities.

With most of the U.S. dates held outdoors, one of the highlights on the domestic leg was a July 13, 1987, benefit at New York's Madison Square Garden, which raised more than $400,000 for AIDS research.

"I don't want to turn this into a morbid event, but AIDS is a painful and mysterious disease that continues to elude us," she told the Garden crowd. Later in the set, she would dedicate "Live to Tell" to the memory of an old friend who was a recent AIDS victim.

While "Live to Tell" was particularly moving that night, the number was arguably the centerpiece throughout the entire Who's That Girl tour. Madonna delivered the song in dramatic style, performing alone on stage beneath a screen that displayed a giant blow-up of her face. Asked how she felt gazing up at the photo every night, she told *Rolling Stone,* "I see it and I say 'Oh, God, what have I done? What have I created? Is that me or is this me, this small person standing down here on the stage?'"

The Who's That Girl Tour finally ended in Turin, Italy, with a show documented in its entirety on the Warner-Reprise home video release, *Ciao Italia!*

With a break from the concert scene in 1988, Madonna took the opportunity to

continued on page 40

"THE BLOND AMBITION TOUR IS A NIFTY SUMMATION OF THE SPECTACLE THAT IS MADONNA, COMBINING CONVINCING MOMENTS OF MUSICAL PERFORMANCE, OVER-THE-TOP STAGE PRODUCTION AND CHOREOGRAPHY WITH A HEALTHY DOSE OF OLD-FASHIONED PROMOTION."

Japanese concert review; *Rolling Stone,* **1990**

Both pages: Few performers are as energetic, imaginative, and tireless as Madonna. Her Blond Ambition dates confirmed the uniqueness of her talent, and her gift for clever self-promotion.

Above: Madonna developed a special rapport with her Blond Ambition dancers. Right: The amusing "Material Girl" number from the Blond tour.

This page: And she plays the harp, too! More images that capture the verve and excitement of the Blond Ambition Tour.

This page: Madonna's backup singers gave her solid support during the Blond Ambition dates. As good as they were, though, Madonna dominated every number.

continued from page 35
make her Broadway bow in the David Mamet play *Speed the Plow*. A longtime admirer of the playwright's work (she had sent him a fan letter after seeing his *House of Games*) Madonna first heard about the new play when she was dining in Manhattan with movie and theater director Mike Nichols, who suggested she audition for the part.

Speed the Plow opened at the Royale Theatre on May 4, 1988, and saw Madonna performing alongside noted actors Ron Silver and Joe Mantegna. Her role was that of an office temp who works for a Hollywood production head. Her boss has made a wager with another man that he can seduce her. It was hardly a glamorous or uplifting part and Madonna eventually succumbed to the strain of playing it.

"I felt the girl I played was extremely defeated," she told *Interview*. "And I felt defeated all summer . . . I didn't feel my usual . . . self." Madonna told the *Advocate*, "I was depressed the whole time I was doing it because Ron and Joe had the good parts. They were victorious in the end, and I felt like a loser at the end of every night. I really felt my part . . . I also knew the critics were hovering over me like vultures waiting to rip me to shreds. It's horrible to go out and do it with that feeling."

In actual fact, her performance drew mixed reviews in the press—some bad,

40

but others quite favorable. The *New York Daily News* seemed quite content to bluntly proclaim, "No, she can't act." However, *New York Times* theater critic Frank Rich, known to be particularly tough on his subjects, gave kudos to Madonna for her "intelligent, scrupulously disciplined comic acting."

Appearing on the E! Entertainment network, co-star Ron Silver concluded, "I thought whatever controversy or criticism she may have gotten was very, very unfair . . . she's a lot smarter than people give her credit for. I think she can be a very good actress and I like her very much." For her part, Madonna maintains that she'll consider a return to Broadway "when a part is offered in a good play."

Madonna's concerts may provide her with the best "parts" of all, which brings us to her Blond Ambition Tour. "It's much more theatrical than anything I've ever done." Speaking to MTV, that's how Madonna described her first road outing since the Who's That Girl Tour—and she wasn't kidding.

The new show boasted four basic themes: love, religion, Dick Tracy, and dance. Madonna's brother, Christopher Ciccone, designed elaborate stage sets that enabled his sister to deliver a potpourri of her musical catalog in more of a Broadway-stylized production than a conventional rock 'n' roll setting. The first set recreated the industrial vibe of the "Express Yourself" video; an Arabian-like bedroom scene was used for a sexy ver-

Madonna looked every inch the classic French lady during the 1990 MTV Awards, even if she didn't exactly act like one!

sion of "Like a Virgin"; songs like "Papa Don't Preach," "Live to Tell," "Oh Father," and "Like a Prayer" were performed in a Catholic church-style setting; and a 1930s ballroom motif was employed for a selection of tunes from the *Dick Tracy* album.

Tour choreographer and co-director Vincent Patterson described the show to *Entertainment Weekly* as "a combination of rock 'n' roll, theater, and Broadway—a real mixed animal. This is Madonna's every fantasy come true. It's one hallucination after another."

Musicians were barely visible on stage, with a nine-member dance troupe gaining much more of the audiences' attention. And, of course, there was Madonna, ruling the roost in her eye-catching Jean-Paul Gaultier-designed costumes.

As is clear in the *Truth or Dare* movie, Madonna enjoyed a particularly close relationship with her dancers on the Blond Ambition Tour. "They were hard workers, extremely talented, but I don't think they were jaded," she later explained to Carrie Fisher for a *Rolling Stone* interview. "They hadn't been on tour with other people and hadn't traveled. They hadn't been associated with—I hate to say the word—'celebrity.' Everything was completely new to them . . . I could show them things and be a mother to them. Take care of them . . . ."

Madonna had found a couple of her best dancers when she was first exposed to "vogueing" in a New York club and chanced upon a group of voguers called the House Of Extravaganza.

"I went to the Sound Factory with my girlfriend Debi M. because I wanted to go dancing," she told writer Don Shewey. "At the time I was trying to visualize things for my show, and I was hanging around a lot of clubs—watching different styles, looking for dancers. I don't like the people who go to [dance] class all the time; they're really boring dancers. I was just looking for some street dancers, you know, and when I saw Jose [Guitierez] and Luis [Camacho] dancing, I was completely blown away."

As with the Who's That Girl Tour, Madonna began her Blond Ambition itinerary in Japan, followed by an extensive U.S. leg. Controversy followed her everywhere, but none more so than in Italy, where various religious and cultural organizations sought to ban the show. Forced to hold a press conference when she arrived at Rome airport, Madonna told reporters, "I'm an Italian-American and proud of it. I ask you fair-minded men and women of the Catholic Church to come see my show and judge for yourself . . . . My show is not a conventional rock concert, but, a theatrical presentation of my music. And, like the theater, it poses questions, provokes thoughts and takes you on an emotional journey."

Emotional, yes, and fascinating, too. Who can say where the on-stage Madonna will take us next?

Above and opposite: Madonna's performance at the 1991 Academy Awards ceremony recalled the memory of the legendary Marilyn Monroe. As powerful a live performer as anyone on the scene today, Madonna seems destined to carve out a legend of her own.

"EXPRESS YOURSELF"
Madonna and Her Movies

I NEVER MET ANYONE WHO HAS

SUCH A FOCUS. SHE GOES RIGHT FOR IT

AND GETS WHAT SHE WANTS. I ADMIRE

THAT A LOT. BUT I THINK BEHIND ALL

THAT IS A LITTLE GIRL INSIDE."

Rosanna Arquette, co-star of *Desperately Seeking Susan;*
***Rolling Stone*, 1985**

The lure of movie stardom means a great deal to Madonna, but her box office record has been spotty. Bloodhounds of Broadway (left) was a flop, while Desperately Seeking Susan (opposite) was a surprise hit.

Madonna's first appearance in a mainstream film was in Vision Quest, *a minor drama in which she had a small part as—guess what?—a singer.*

DESPITE THE FACT THAT SHE HAS appeared in several major motion pictures, silver screen success has thus far eluded Madonna—and she's the first to admit it.

"I've been a failure so far and the reason is I simply haven't put a lot of thought into it," she told a reporter from the *Los Angeles Times* in May 1991. "I haven't honored or respected a movie career the way I should have—I didn't approach it in the way I approached my music career . . . and I underestimated the power of the medium."

Madonna's first foray into the film world was in the early '80s, while she was struggling to break into the music business. Answering an ad for what she hoped might be "an interesting art film," the singer connected with New York University student Stephen Lewicki, who immediately cast her in his production, *A Certain Sacrifice*. Written, produced, and directed by Lewicki, the project turned out to be little more than a low-budget, soft porn flick. Madonna reportedly earned $100 for starring in the picture but her association with Lewicki would come back to haunt her.

In 1985, while Madonna was riding high on the multi-platinum success of *Like a Virgin*, Lewicki cashed in on her stardom by cutting a deal for the home video release of *A Certain Sacrifice*. Despite a court appeal, Madonna was unable to stop the video from hitting store shelves.

Madonna made her "legitimate" screen debut in February 1985 with a brief appearance in the Jon Peters-produced *Vision Quest*. Her tiny cameo as a nightclub singer did little for her acting resume, but she did score Top 10 hits with "Crazy For You" and "The Gambler," her contributions to the Geffen soundtrack.

A month later, Madonna garnered greater onscreen visibility with the Susan Seidelman-directed *Desperately Seeking Susan*. In this mystery/black comedy about confused identities, Madonna was perfectly cast as a streetwise Manhattan schemer opposite Rosanna Arquette's naive New Jersey housewife. Shot in New York toward the end of 1984 on a modest budget, the film turned a tidy profit for Orion Pictures, which took full advantage of Madonna's musical success in its marketing campaign. Co-star Arquette had been somewhat peeved when a scene was written to incorporate a new Madonna song ("Into The Groove") and she was understandably livid when the studio gave MTV a video that comprised footage from the film focusing mainly on Madonna.

For her part, the singer was well aware that Orion was exploiting her pop stardom to promote its picture. She also knew that her musical career would gain invaluable exposure from heavy MTV airplay of "Into The Groove." Still, there was a downside, as she told *Rolling Stone*:

"It's really a drag because I'm trying to establish myself as an actress, not as a singer making movies." Madonna garnered

This page: Madonna came into her own as a film personality with Desperately Seeking Susan. Funny and spontaneous, Madonna dominated every scene she was in.

This page: Good casts and good intentions don't guarantee a good movie. In spite of the on-screen pairing of Madonna and her husband, Sean Penn, Shanghai Surprise *was an embarrassing critical and box-office flop.*

positive critical response for her performance in *Desperately Seeking Susan*. However, cynics suggested that her role called for little more than "simply showing up on the set and being herself" and that she had yet to prove her true acting abilities.

"A truly miserable experience" is how Madonna describes the filming of her next movie, *Shanghai Surprise*, a Handmade Films production in which she co-starred with her then-husband Sean Penn. Based on the novel *Faraday's Flowers* by Tony Kenrick, the film told the tale of a prim-and-proper young missionary from Massachusetts, who travels to the Orient and falls in love with a small-time grifter.

"We didn't actually plan on working on the film together," Madonna explained at a press conference. "Sean had just finished a film and was looking for another movie to do and I'd just finished working on my record and I was looking for a movie to do. I read the script and loved it and asked him to read it for his opinion. He also liked the male role, so we looked at each other and thought maybe this would be a good one to do together."

Big mistake. Married less than six months when they set off for China in January 1986, the Penns enjoyed a brief stint on location in the city of Shanghai. However, all hell broke loose when they left the mainland and moved on to Hong Kong. During their stay in the British colony, the couple was hounded mercilessly by the paparazzi and the situation worsened when shooting continued in London. Ex-Beatle and Handmade Films' boss George Harrison begged the press to back off, but the damage had already been done.

Making matters worse was the fact that director Jim Goddard (recommended by actor Martin Sheen for his work on the *Kennedy* TV mini-series), simply could not pull the picture together.

Not surprisingly, the critics skewered *Shanghai Surprise*. The *1986 Film Yearbook* branded it a "Turkey of the Year," and dubbed the rickshaw-chase scene "as thrilling as watching mushrooms grow."

After the *Shanghai* fiasco, Madonna's next movie was to have been the Tri-Star production, *Blind Date*. That deal reportedly fell through when she discovered that the studio had not sought her approval before hiring Bruce Willis as the film's leading man. With Kim Basinger taking the *Blind Date* part opposite Willis, Madonna eventually signed on to co-star with Griffin Dunne (*After Hours*) in *Slammer*. The project was brought to her by James Foley, who had directed her husband, Sean Penn, in *At Close Range*, and had subsequently worked on her "Live To Tell" and "Papa Don't Preach" videos.

"Jim knew I'd wanted to do a comedy for so long," said Madonna. Her role was that of a smart but kooky gal named Nikki Finn, out on parole after four years in jail for a murder she did not commit and determined to find out who had framed her.

This page: Madonna co-starred with the talented Griffin Dunne in Who's That Girl?, *but this picture, too, died at the box office, and failed to impress critics.*

Top and above: Bloodhounds of Broadway *allowed Madonna to cultivate still another sort of look. Unfortunately, poor promotion and nonexistent audience response doomed the film to video-store obscurity. By this time, Madonna's film career looked to be in trouble.*

After principal shooting on *Slammer* was completed in February 1987, the film's title was changed to *Who's That Girl?* and a release date was set for August 7. A press release described Madonna's character as "a feisty, free-spirited femme destined to take her place among the screen's great comic heroines." To be sure, Madonna's performance was a lively one that marked her best screen work to date. But nothing could stop the movie from taking a major nose-dive at the box office. In its first nine days of release, *Who's That Girl?* took in a disastrous $5.1 million; Madonna must have been beginning to wonder how on earth she was going to make her mark in the movies.

In 1989 Madonna made a brief film appearance as a nightclub singer in *Bloodhounds of Broadway*, a period piece based on four stories by Damon Runyan. Despite a credible cast that also included Matt Dillon, Jennifer Grey, Julie Hagerty, and Randy Quaid, the film bypassed theaters and went straight into video stores, where it gathered dust on the shelves. Blink and you would have missed this one.

Bloodhounds of Broadway had a low-key vibe, but Madonna's next film was just the opposite. By the time *Dick Tracy* opened nationally on June 15, 1990, the hype for Walt Disney's $23 million entry into the summer sweepstakes was totally overwhelming.

Madonna starred as torch-singing temptress Breathless Mahoney opposite director/leading man Warren Beatty, with whom she began a much-publicized off-screen fling during production. According to Madonna, Beatty took a year to make up his mind before agreeing to cast her as Breathless. (Melanie Griffith had reportedly been a contender for the part.) Once Madonna had snagged the part, she garnered no preferential on-set treatment from her beau. "Warren insisted that I get fatter," she told *Premiere* magazine. "He wanted to pour me into my dresses. I gained ten pounds . . . . I had to bleach my hair blond again, pluck my eyebrows. It was traumatic to get the hair right. Hair is the most important thing to Warren. He would walk around me like a vulture, making me feel like the ugliest thing in the world. And the dresses . . . he'd say 'tighter, tighter, cut it down lower.' I felt like a mannequin, a slab of beef. I was treated that way on the set—the lust factor."

An amusing shooting anecdote came from make-up man John Caglione, Jr., who was extremely worried when Madonna's breasts had to be glued to her tight-fitting gown in order to achieve the visual effect Beatty wanted. Caglione's mind was spinning: "What if she has an allergic reaction to the glue? What if we discolor a breast? Not only will we be sued, we'll become known as the schmucks who destroyed a national treasure!"

Madonna's performance in *Dick Tracy* called for her to sing a few tunes, includ-

This page: Dick Tracy was a big hit in the summer of 1990, and recharged Madonna's drive to succeed in movies. She's seen above with Mandy Patinkin and at left with a heavily made-up Al Pacino.

ing the Oscar-winning Stephen Sondheim composition "Sooner Or Later." However, in retrospect, she has mixed feelings about the picture.

"I have to admit I've never really seen the movie," she confessed in an *L.A. Calendar* interview. "I saw a lot of bits of pieces and I did see an early cut. And I saw about half of it at a premiere in Washington, D.C., but then I had to leave. You could say I have a lot of unresolved feelings about it. I remember being very upset that all my big music scenes were cut up the way they were. . . . I learned a lot about filmmaking from Warren but obviously it didn't make me a big box office star, did it?"

Madonna's next film, *Truth or Dare*, was a Hollywood rarity: a feature-length documentary about an active star. To top it off, the film ignited controversy from the first day of release. Madonna remarked, "Everyone overreacts to everything I do. So I can just imagine the overreactions to this. . . ." With scenes that included visiting her mother's grave, the shunning of her inebriated brother, exposing her breasts, and lying in bed with seven young men in various stages of undress, Madonna knew full well that *Truth or Dare* would cause more than her usual commotion.

When she initially decided to film some of her 1990 Blond Ambition Tour, the concept had been little more than to capture the visual and aural excitement of her live performances. It wasn't long,

though, before Madonna decided to turn the project into a no-holds-barred, behind-the-scenes look at life on the tour. As she told *Rolling Stone*, the decision to go beyond the boundaries of a standard rockumentary owed a good deal to the close rapport she had established with her entourage, particularly the dancers.

"Before we even got on the road I started developing a relationship with my dancers, and I was so fascinated with them that I thought: 'No, I don't want to make a movie about the show . . . I want to make a movie about us, about our life."

Orginally conceived as a TV special, the project was to have been directed by David Fincher, with whom Madonna had worked on a couple of her short-form videos. When Fincher pulled out of the live shoot, Madonna turned to handsome 26-year-old director Alek Keshishian, just three days before the tour kicked off in Japan.

Madonna had first become aware of Keshishian several years earlier, when she saw a rock musical adaptation of Emily Brontë's *Wuthering Heights*. The musical, which featured some of Madonna's music, had been undertaken by Keshishian while he was studying at Harvard. Eager to work on a feature film, Keshishian had gone on to shoot videos for the likes of Bobby Brown and Elton John. However, he harbored a serious desire to work with Madonna, as he explained to *Vanity Fair*:

"I said to myself, 'Go on with your

Above and opposite: Truth or Dare *is a remarkable blend of autobiography, psychodrama, and performance film. In all, it offers an intimate and frequently funny portrait of a unique star.*

Truth or Dare, *directed by Alek Keshishian, reveals more than just Madonna's body. The film gets to the core of her personality, and takes a particularly hard look at her need to be in control of every aspect of her life.*

[Keshishian's] videos; I'd seen him around in nightclubs and stuff; I liked the people he was with; I liked the way he looked; I liked the way he danced; I knew he was educated; and I felt that I had something in common with him. So I just called him."

Keshishian shot more than 250 hours of film for *Truth or Dare*, using color for concert footage and black-and-white for offstage camerawork. According to Madonna, the director deserves tremendous credit for his insistence on keeping the camera rolling, when others might have given up in their attempts to truly capture the feel of life on the road with a superstar.

"I was very wary of Alek, I just didn't trust him," she told *The Face*. "In this type of situation, you either become very close to someone or you hate them more than life itself. It was really difficult for me in the beginning because I didn't know what I was getting into. By the end he could come into the bathroom with me. I didn't care. But it's completely to his credit that I grew relaxed in front of the camera."

The decision to transform the project from television to movie screens was reached when a deal was struck with Miramax Films, the hot independent studio run by brothers Bob and Harvey Weinstein. What prompted Miramax to get involved? "Madonna, of course," Harvey Weinstein told *Venice* magazine. "I met with her when she and Alek were shooting in New York. She was honest

life, Alek. You are not going to work with Madonna.' And then out of the blue, one afternoon at the end of March last year, the phone rings and it's Madonna asking me to do this."

For her part, Madonna told *Entertainment Weekly*, "I'd seen a lot of

and smart and promised a no-holds-barred look at the world of celebrity. She kept her word."

After New York and Los Angeles screenings to benefit AIDS research, *Truth or Dare* had its national opening on May 10, 1991. For once, it seemed that Madonna had done something to satisfy critics, who generally gave the film a thumbs-up response. More importantly, the film enjoyed a successful opening at box offices.

"This movie is worth five years of psychoanalysis. I really got to know myself," Madonna told *The Face*. And of the film's final montage featuring her frolicking in bed with her dancers, she noted, "In two minutes it underlines what you've

just seen in two hours. It's my need to be loved but also my need to be in charge."

Almost simultaneous with the release of *Truth or Dare*, Madonna went to work opposite Tom Hanks in director Penny Marshall's *A League of Their Own*, a film about female baseball players in the 1940s. In addition, Madonna may or may not be seen as an acrobat in a new Woody Allen film, depending on whether the director decides to retain her footage. Additionally, her name is still hotly linked to a movie version of the Andrew Lloyd Webber musical *Evita*. Madonna as the wife of a South American dictator? She has pronounced, "If there is an 'Evita,' I contend that I will be her." Keep your eyes peeled, film fans.

Top: Madonna with her Blond Ambition backup singers, Nikki Harris and Donna Delory. Above: The star arrives at New York's Ziegfeld Theatre for the premiere of Truth or Dare.

"Open Your Heart"
Madonna and Her Men

I'M NOT EXACTLY SURE WHO I'M

LOOKING FOR. I WISH I KNEW. . . . I

WONDER IF I COULD FIND SOMEONE LIKE

ME . . . [LAUGHS] IF I DID I WOULD

PROBABLY KILL THEM."

Madonna; *Vanity Fair*, 1991

The many men in Madonna's life run the gamut from her brother Christopher (left) to her ex-husband, film star Sean Penn (opposite).

WHEN ASKED TO NAME THE LOVE of her life during a scene in the movie *Truth or Dare*, Madonna gets right to the point with a one-word answer: "Sean."

The Sean in question is, of course, actor Sean Penn, whom she married in 1985 but then divorced less than four years later. "I still love Sean and I understand very clearly, now that time has passed, why things didn't work out between us," Madonna told *Q* magazine in June 1991.

"I did have a real connection with Sean and I still do," she added. "I feel close to him even though we're not physically close. Going through what we went through made us very close. There was a lot of pressure. I mean, it really is amazing we didn't kill each other. But I don't feel like it was a waste of time."

Madonna met Penn while shooting the video for "Material Girl" in early 1985. Previously, her name had been romantically linked with mainly music-oriented lads, including Stephen Bray, Dan Gilroy, and DJ John "Jellybean" Benitez.

Reflecting on her courtship with Penn in *Rolling Stone*, Madonna stated, "It was a really romantic thing. We were madly in love with each other, and we decided quite soon after we were seeing each other that we were going to get married."

Indeed, just seven months after their first meeting, on August 16, 1985, Madonna and Sean tied the knot at a cliffside house in Malibu. However, right from that wedding day, the marriage would be under the savage and ever-watchful eye of the press.

"I didn't think I was going to be getting married with thirteen helicopters flying over my head," Madonna told *Rolling Stone*. "It turned into a circus."

In addition to the helicopters, Sean reportedly got into a scuffle with a photographer, who had gatecrashed his way into the reception. Penn's bouts of fisticuffs with the paparazzi would be well documented over the next few years.

Madonna also told *Rolling Stone* that she felt the press "really went out of their way to pick on Sean, to the point where they would walk down the street and kind of poke at him and say, 'C'mon, c'mon, hit me, hit me'. . . ."

Madonna would not condone Penn's violent scuffles, but as she later told *Vanity Fair*, "Sean was very protective of me. I liked his public demonstrations of protecting me. In retrospect, I understand why he dealt with the press the way he did, but you have to realize it's a losing battle."

During the marriage, Madonna and Sean would be dubbed the Poison Penns by the tabloid press, which seemed hell-bent on destroying the union. Madonna has been quoted as saying, "There were rumors about us getting a divorce a week after the wedding."

The press may have brought a lot of unpleasantness to the relationship, but

The press has been interested in all of Madonna's men, but actor Sean Penn inspired the most feverish coverage of all. Here, Madonna assumes an uncharacteristically camera-shy attitude to match Penn's.

Madonna and Sean clearly had a lot of their own behind-closed-doors problems that would ultimately lead to their separation. Madonna has told the press that the collapse of their marriage had "a slow breaking point." However, an apparent violent outburst by Penn in their Malibu home caused her to file a complaint of assault against her husband on December 28, 1988. Those charges were later dropped, but within a week Madonna filed for divorce, citing "irreconcilable differences."

Naturally, interviewers were keen to discuss the downfall of her marriage when Madonna faced the press to publicize her 1989 album, *Like a Prayer.* She was reluctant to go into much detail but did note that she and Sean were "two fires rubbing up against each other."

Madonna refused to badmouth her ex-husband publicly, but she later confessed that she "went through a hostile period" and that her "heart was really broken."

And then came actor Warren Beatty . . . . Shortly after Madonna and the veteran Hollywood Casanova began discussing the possibility of her acting in his *Dick Tracy* movie, the couple was rumored to be having a love affair. And by the time the publicity wheels for the movie were rolling, Madonna and Warren made no secret of their romance.

During his long career, the handsome Beatty has been linked with a string of famous ladies, including Joan Collins, Brigitte Bardot, Julie Christie, Diane Keaton, and Isabelle Adjani. "Madonna is more famous than any of them," noted writer Bill Zehme in an interesting analy-

Madonna's August 16, 1985, marriage to Penn was an opulent affair that was gatecrashed by the press, and even buzzed by helicopters.

59

Madonna with model/actor Tony Ward . . .

. . . with a fellow introduced by Madonna as "my new boyfriend . . .

. . . and with pop superstar Michael Jackson.

sis of their relationship that introduced his Beatty interview in *Rolling Stone*. "She is more famous than he is; she is more famous than everyone, more or less," Zehme continued. "By loving him, she makes him more famous than he was before. Theirs' is a sort of vampire love: She needs his credibility; he needs her youth. He is fifty-three, and she is thirty-one, and they are evenly matched legends: hers is louder, his is longer. It works out. . . ."

Madonna dubbed Beatty "old man," while his pet name for her was "buzzbomb." The affair that reportedly began during her divorce proceedings finally fizzled out sometime after the release of *Dick Tracy* and during the Blond Ambition Tour. Madonna claims that she and Beatty are still friendly.

Since her affair with Beatty, Madonna had a brief fling with model/actor Tony Ward, who appeared with her in the controversial "Justify My Love" video. Rumors abound that this union collapsed after the British tabloid press announced that Ward had secretly wed another gal after meeting Madonna. This time there may have been some truth in the scuttlebutt, because a marriage license was known to exist.

With the exception of Ward, things were generally low-key on Madonna's romantic front during 1991—or publicly, at least. During the wave of interviews to

"MADONNA IS SIMULTANEOUS-
LY TOUCHING AND MORE FUN
THAN A BARREL OF MONKEYS.
SHE'S FUNNY AND SHE'S GIFT-
ED IN SO MANY AREAS AND
HAS THE KIND OF ENERGY AS
A PERFORMER THAT CAN'T
HELP BUT MAKE YOU
ENGAGED."

Warren Beatty; *Rolling Stone,* **1990**

*The men, like the hits, keep on com-
ing. Madonna flexes for rapper
Vanilla Ice . . .*

promote *Truth or Dare,* she claimed that
she was very much a single girl. In light
of some of her comments in these interviews, one can't help but feel that she
longs for certain aspects of marriage, but
recognizes that a married relationship may
be difficult for someone in her position.

"There's something to be said for a
domestic life and knowing somebody's
there for you," she told the *Advocate.* "I
just think it's hard to live the life I lead
and then have this happily married life. I
haven't been successful at it so far, but
who's to say I can't be?"

Madonna added that she has yet to
meet someone who could "take all of me
ultimately, who I think is my intellectual
equal and truly understands me."

Does she have any interest in babies?
"As soon as I find Mr. Right—No, as
soon as I finish just one more project!"

. . . snuggles with Truth or Dare
director Alek Keshishian . . .

. . . and makes the scene with Dick
Tracy *co-star Warren Beatty.*

"CAUSING A COMMOTION"
Madonna On The Scene

W
HAT A TRAMP!"

Front-page headline; *New York Post,* **1991**

Madonna's more humorless critics may not like her image, but to legions of young fans like those at the left, she's a role model they can have fun with. Even from the earliest period of her stardom (opposite), Madonna managed to make a splash wherever she went.

The many looks of Madonna. Here, saucy and scruffy, early in her career.

Surprise! She can be coolly sophisticated, too. Some of her fans have mixed feelings about the dark hair.

Back in the blonde mode once again, and looking very much like Marilyn Monroe, circa 1962.

Intensely elegant, a look quite appropriate for New York City.

The street urchin, from Madonna's Desperately Seeking Susan *period.*

The ethereal Madonna, pastel-pretty.

Stunning in the classic "little black dress."

The casual look, for a night on the town.

Prim and proper, as befits the missionary she played in Shanghai Surprise.

Madonna sets out to disprove the old chestnut about girls who wear glasses.

Well-scrubbed and athletic during the "Papa Don't Preach" shoot.

Madonna makes even a bathrobe look good in this backstage shot taken during the Blond Ambition Tour.

Left: Never a shrinking violet, Madonna made a typically theatrical entrance at this 1990 opening.

Photos right: At the 1991 Cannes Film Festival, Madonna went from demure to daring in a flash.

Photos left: Madonna turned up the voltage at a Los Angeles Dance-A-Thon that benefited AIDS research.

Right: The AIDS benefit illustrates Madonna's gift for combining publicity with her desire to do charitable work.

MIDWAY THROUGH THE TELL-ALL movie *Truth or Dare* there is a wonderful backstage scene where Madonna is in her dressing room with Warren Beatty as her tired, overworked larynx is checked by a throat specialist. As the cameras continue to roll during the examination, an incredulous Beatty inquires, "Does anyone talk about how crazy this is?"

When the doctor asks Madonna if she would prefer to talk off-camera, Beatty instantly quips, "She doesn't want to live off-camera, much less talk!"

"Warren is very shy and private and he doesn't understand my lack of inhibition because he's the opposite of me," Madonna would later tell *Q* magazine. "The point of that scene is that it serves to show how different Warren and I are."

Indeed, unlike the shy and reclusive Beatty, Madonna truly loves to be in the camera's eye—not that she has much choice in the matter, mind you. No matter where she goes—movie premieres, charity events, award ceremonies, restaurants, nightclubs, or even just jogging in the park—the photographers hound after her every move.

Rather than put up a fruitless fight for her privacy, Madonna learned from the outset of her career that she would ultimately exercise more control over her image by giving the paparazzi what they wanted. In many respects, Madonna herself created the legend that is Madonna.

For example, when it was announced that she would be appearing at the 1991

Madonna's friendship with the unorthodox actress/comic Sandra Bernhardt has piqued the interest of both stars' fans.

Academy Awards ceremony, tongues were wagging over who would be her date for the night. After all, her affair with Beatty and a fling with model/actor Tony Ward were over. And unless the press had miraculously failed to link her with a new beau, Madonna was arguably the world's hottest single girl. So who did she finally show up with on Oscar night? None other than her male counterpart in the pop world, megastar Michael Jackson. And no matter how many Oscars were handed out to Kevin Costner, the must-shoot photo of the night award belonged to Madonna and Jackson.

But what was she doing with him? Were they just good friends? Could the pair have romantic ties? Perhaps there was a work project in the pipeline? Madonna knew full well that she would cause a major commotion by hanging out with Jackson.

Just for the record, were they up to anything?

"We're considering working on a song together," Madonna revealed to the *Advocate*. "I would like to completely redo [Michael's] image," she continued. "But I'm not going to get together and do some stupid ballad or love duet—no one's going to buy it, first of all. I said, 'Look Michael, if you want to do something with me, you have to be willing to go all the way or I'm not going to do it.' He keeps saying yes. . . ."

These days, to be seated with Jackson in the front row at the biggest show business event of the year is something Madonna probably takes in her stride. But being at the center of such a stellar scenario would have been pure fantasy for the little girl who grew up in Michigan idolizing Hollywood stars. Even from an early age, though, Madonna thrived on getting attention. She remarked to *Rolling Stone*, "I knew I had to be extra special, super-charming to get what I wanted, 'cause I grew up with a lot of brothers and sisters and we had to share everything. I did all I could to really stand out, and that nurtured a lot of confidence and drive and ambition."

As a dance student during her teens, Madonna made sure she got noticed by showing up to class in less-than-conventional attire. Sometimes, she'd even take off her top and exercise in just a brassiere.

"I was a real ham," she confessed to *Rolling Stone*. "I did everything I could to get attention and be the opposite of everyone else. I'd rip my leotards and wear teeny little safety pins. And I'd run my tights. . . . I could have gone to a nightclub right after class."

Unlike many pop stars for whom puppet-like styling is necessary, Madonna always knew how to create an image for herself—one that would not go unnoticed. During a recent interview with *Entertainment Weekly*, top fashion photographer Herb Ritts recalled his first meeting with the superstar:

"The first time I worked with her was when I was doing the poster for *Desperately Seeking Susan*. She marched in with this little cigar box full of jewels and trinkets that she wanted to wear. She knew exactly how she wanted to look. I liked that."

By the time the 1985 Virgin Tour was rolling, Madonna's "look" had become so fashionable that it inspired a nation of young female "wannabes" to emulate her style.

Reflecting on public reaction to her appearance, Madonna told *Rolling Stone*, "I was in control of everything I was doing and I think when people realized that, it confused them. The fact that I was wearing those clothes was meant to drive home the point that you can be sexy and strong at the same time. In a way it was necessary to wear the clothes."

During that period, the publication in *Playboy* and *Penthouse* of photographs showing the *unclothed* Madonna was something the artist could not prevent. As she later told *Rolling Stone*, "When I first found out

Top and above: Recording success has brought Madonna numerous industry awards. These ceremonies, such as the 1985 and '87 American Music Awards, have also provided her with a chance to vary her look.

Left and right: Does Madonna ever make an unescorted entrance? Rarely. Anyway, eye-catching outfits such as these are not designed for evenings spent in solitude.

Right: Hearts 'n' flowers dominate this Love Ball evening of Madonna-style romance.

Left: Madonna brought the classic elegance of pearls to this 1991 Los Angeles function.

Left: Madonna with designer Jean-Paul Gaultier; she looks every inch the movie star she is determined to become. Right: Dancing with abandon at a party in L.A.

about it, the thing that annoyed me most wasn't so much that they were nude photographs but that I felt really out of control—for the first time in what I thought to be several years of careful planning and knowing what was going to happen. It took me by surprise."

The nude photos came out of a brief stint Madonna spent as a model for photography students in the late '70s, shortly after she had moved to New York. Czechoslovakian lensman Martin Hugo Maximilian Schreiber recently published his collection (comprising many of the shots that surfaced in '85) in a book titled *Madonna Nudes 1979*. For her February 12, 1979, session with Schreiber, Madonna earned a paltry $30.

In the introduction to his book, Schreiber notes, "She was a determined young woman. She was strong emotionally and she had ambition. I felt that nothing or anyone was going to stand in her way. At the time, I don't remember her saying anything about singing. That came later."

These days, Madonna has no problem being photographed in various forms of undress. But, for her, the key word is always "control." Working with a select, close-knit group of photographers, Madonna loves to tantalize and shock. But, unlike those early nudes, she maintains total control over what the public will ultimately see. Give them what they want, but always leave them wanting just a little bit more—that would appear to be her modus operandi.

Critics of The Tonight Show *may claim that host Johnny Carson has lost his hipness, but he was sharp enough to invite Madonna onto the show in 1987.*

"I LOVE BLOND HAIR BUT IT REALLY DOES SOMETHING DIFFERENT TO YOU. I FEEL MORE GROUNDED WHEN I HAVE DARK HAIR, AND I FEEL MORE ETHEREAL WHEN I HAVE LIGHT HAIR. I ALSO FEEL MORE ITALIAN WHEN MY HAIR IS DARK. . . ."

Madonna; *Rolling Stone,* **1989**

Similarly, she will allow herself to engage in in-depth, often highly candid interviews. But she and longtime press representative, Liz Rosenberg, have mastered the art of knowing just when and where to press the right journalistic buttons. While promoting *Truth or Dare*, for example, Madonna engaged in an R-rated chat with the gay/lesbian publication the *Advocate*, knowing full well that some of her outspoken, "shocking" comments would be picked up and reprinted in newspapers and magazines around the world. Thus, Madonna was able to control her own sensationalist press.

Indeed, reporters find it hard to dig up much scandal about Madonna since she tends to do such a fine job of creating her own. She is often the source of rumors about her; she has been quoted as saying that she likes to "push people's buttons."

"I'm not addicted to scandal," she said in the *Advocate* interview. "I feel that I'm on a mission to educate people. When I say 'pushing people's buttons,' I mean really making them see things and making them feel things they're not necessarily comfortable with feeling. It's not just 'Oh, I want to be scandalous.'"

In that same interview, Madonna revealed another reason why she is able to control much of what comes out in the press: "Everyone that is employed by me signs a privacy contract, from my maid to a back-up singer. It's a way of protecting myself before I get to know people and know that I can trust them."

And what of Madonna's private life? What does she do when she's not in the public eye?

Fact is, Madonna is very rarely off-the-scene. Clearly a workaholic, she never allows herself much time to relax. Word has it that she has been on vacation only about three times during the past decade and, on each occasion, she reportedly went along more to appease a current love interest than out of her own burning desire for sun and sand.

Madonna keeps homes in both New York and Los Angeles, the two cities where she does most of her work when she's not touring or filming. Her seven-room Manhattan apartment is located on a well-to-do block near Central Park. However, its location has become so well known to both the paparazzi and fans that there are always people hanging around outside when she is in town. They hope that their vigil will be rewarded by a glimpse of the star, or a quick photo.

The constant presence of fans and photographers doesn't seem to faze Madonna. According to one fan, she once said, "I don't mind if you sit outside my house, but don't follow me. I just want to go for a walk. I'm a regular person and want to be left alone sometimes."

"I ABSOLUTELY CAN'T EVER GO OUT IN LONDON. I CAN'T TAKE A WALK DOWN THE STREET OR GO TO A MUSEUM OR GO SHOPPING AND THAT'S A DRAG."

Madonna; *Q* magazine, 1991

The inside of her Manhattan pad, reportedly renovated and decorated by her brother, Christopher, in an early French deco style, is said to house a fine art collection that includes paintings by Tamara de Lempicka, Fernand Leger, Picasso, and Dali, as well as photographs by Andre Kertesz and Edward Weston. Similarly, a lot of artwork was on display at her house in the Hollywood Hills, where electronically controlled wrought-iron gates granted her more privacy from the outside world. Madonna's new Bel Air home, an $8 million French villa that she purchased in the summer of 1991, will doubtless have a similar artistic ambience.

Many of Madonna's *Truth or Dare* interviews were conducted at the Hollywood Hills house; the *Advocate* described the home as "the L.A. equiva-

In its heyday, The Tonight Show *could make the careers of hopeful young performers, but when Madonna schmoozed with Johnny, it was she who was bestowing the gift of stardom.*

Opposite: In this unusual, hyper-glamorous image, Madonna makes beauty seem easy.

This page: In reality, Madonna works hard to maintain her figure and good health. But even when exercising, she's surrounded by an entourage.

lent of an apartment on [New York City's] upper West Side. It has the provisional feel of many Hollywood stars' homes . . . the patio, the pool, the spectacular view. But the interior seems art-directed rather than designed for living."

According to *Entertainment Weekly* writer James Kaplan, "The art is beautiful and eclectic but, like its owner, dark and challenging. A consistent theme in paintings, photographs and books is the female nude."

Among the art that was housed in Madonna's Hollywood home were numerous black-and-white photographs by the likes of Kertesz, Weston, Man Ray, and Herb Ritz. Above the fireplace in the main lounge was a work by Leger from the 1930s and a disturbing self-portrait by Mexican artist Frida Kahlo. The ceiling was adorned by a huge 17th century Langlois work depicting three nudes.

These are expensive fancies that Madonna is well able to afford. In October 1990 *Forbes* magazine estimated that Madonna had earned about $125 million since 1986. The front-cover image on that issue's cover was captioned, "America's smartest business woman?"

Well, what does all that money mean to Madonna? "I continue to feel guilty about it like I don't deserve to have it, or something, even though I work really hard," she told *Q* magazine.

According to the star, the guilt factor stems from the fact that she came from a family that never really had much money.

It was a double shot of beauty when Madonna made a personal appearance with Rosanna Arquette, her co-star in Desperately Seeking Susan.

"THERE'S A LOT OF BUSINESS STUFF, BUT THAT DIDN'T COME AS A SURPRISE. BESIDES, I LOVE MEETINGS WITH SUITS . . . BECAUSE I KNOW THEY HAD A REALLY BORING WEEK AND I WALK IN THERE WITH MY ORANGE VELVET LEGGINGS AND DROP POPCORN IN MY CLEAVAGE AND THEN FISH IT OUT AND EAT IT. I LIKE THAT. I KNOW I'M ENTERTAINING THEM AND I KNOW THAT THEY KNOW."

Madonna; *Vanity Fair,* **1991**

"I feel sometimes that someone will come and take it all away from me. That makes me work really hard, all the time."

A major part of Madonna's hard work is her unceasing round of personal appearances at all manner of functions: premieres, benefits, award ceremonies, dinners. On top of this are parties, frantic activity at dance clubs, and mundane events like jogging and walking from a doorway to a waiting car. Inevitably, she is surrounded by her bodyguards, by fans and hangers-on, and by the press. Always, the press. It's a strenuous, very public existence, with the star's every move, every step, every gesture and expression captured by the cameras.

The first half of 1991 saw Madonna hard at work promoting her *Truth or Dare* movie. In addition to press interviews, she attended charity screenings and launch parties in Hollywood and Manhattan.

By the time *Truth or Dare* opened in U.S. theaters, Madonna had jetted off to the annual Cannes Film Festival in the south of France, to hype the film's overseas release. Not surprisingly, she was hounded by the world press during the trip. Undeniably the star of the event, Madonna was quite happy to play up to the paparazzi, particularly when she "daringly" revealed her lingerie to lensmen during her grand entrance to the *Truth or Dare* screening. That cleverly executed move would be broadcast on TV news programs across the globe.

During the festival, Madonna stayed in a private apartment at the exclusive Eden Roc hotel at Cap d'Antibes, some 15 minutes east of Cannes. There, she held her final *Truth or Dare* interview session, a mini-press conference with representatives of four newspapers from England, Australia, Belgium, and Scandinavia.

"[Cannes] has its good points and its bad points," the *Sydney Sun-Herald* reported Madonna as saying. "It takes a long time to drive anywhere but we do get a police escort sometimes and that's good— we get to go through all the red lights!"

After discussing the making of her movie, Madonna was asked if she has maintained a close bond with the Blond Ambition dancers.

"Absolutely," she replied. "We are very close. When I'm in New York, I spend time with the New York dancers, when I'm in L.A., the same. And I'm helping all of them with their various careers, giving them advice, whatever. We are still quite a family and I'm pleased about that. I love them."

The interviewers concluded their allocated session with the superstar by posing a series of more human interest/lifestyle-oriented questions. They asked Madonna if she fears growing old.

"I'm afraid of growing old, but only because I'm a very physical person," she admitted. "I love to run and dance, I'm full of energy and would hate to think of a day that would come when I couldn't do all of those things. But I guess I would have to accept it. That's life . . . ."

And has Madonna changed in the last few years?

"Absolutely. I'm just growing up. I've become more tolerant of myself and other people, I suppose. A couple of years ago, I would not have maybe entertained the idea of having a child or be interested in being tolerant or accepting. . . . I'm more patient I suppose—Hmm, not that much more patient. I hope I'm growing up."

Madonna will continue to "grow up," to change. For now, her presence is an event. In truth, Madonna herself is an event. In an era where celebrities' lives are conducted in newspapers, magazines, and TV-news clips, Madonna's life may be the most public of all. She belongs to the world.

What becomes a legend most? A meeting with another legend! Madonna spends time with the ageless Martha Graham, choreographer par excellence.

Right and below: Madonna leads a life that is remarkably public. Her presence can turn the most mundane scene into an event.

Right: Madonna relies on her personal bodyguard, Clay, for security and protection when out in public. Opposite: For its part, the public can't get enough of Madonna, even in London.

Fame does not come without a price tag. When all the hubbub that surrounds a personal appearance is over, Madonna often departs alone.

Even private moments of joy become public property. No aspect of Madonna's life goes unexamined.

"YOU HAVE TO BE PREPARED FOR YOUR PRIVATE LIFE TO BE SPILLED TO THE WORLD BECAUSE THE MINUTE YOU START GOING OUT WITH ME, THAT'S WHAT HAPPENS."

Madonna; Q magazine, 1991